THE SUN-FISH

EILÉAN NÍ CHUILLEANÁIN

THE SUN-FISH

WAKE FOREST

UNIVERSITY PRESS

Published simultaneously in paperback
and in a clothbound edition
First North American edition published 2010

Wake Forest University Press
Post Office Box 7333
Winston-Salem, NC 27109
www.wfu.edu/wfupress
Designed by Quemadura and typeset
in Bodoni and New Caledonia
Sunfish illustration on page 66
courtesy of Helen Zhu
Printed in the United States of America
LCCN 2010930371
ISBN (clothbound) 978-1-930630-53-6
ISBN (paperback) 978-1-930630-52-9
First published in Ireland
by The Gallery Press

CONTENTS

TO NIALL WOODS AND XENYA OSTROVSKAIA,
MARRIED IN DUBLIN ON 9.IX.09

When you look out across the fields
And you both see the same star
Pitching its tent on the point of the steeple—
That is the time to set out on your journey,
With half a loaf and your mother's blessing.

Leave behind the places that you knew:
All that you leave behind you will find once more,
You will find it in the stories;
The sleeping beauty in her high tower
With her talking cat asleep
Solid beside her feet—you will see her again.

When the cat wakes up he will speak in Irish and Russian
And every night he will tell you a different tale
About the firebird that stole the golden apples,
Gone every morning out of the emperor's garden,
And about the King of Ireland's Son and the Enchanter's Daughter.

The story the cat does not know is the Book of Ruth
And I have no time to tell you how she fared
When she went out at night and she was afraid,
In the beginning of the barley harvest,
Or how she trusted to strangers and stood by her word:

You will have to trust me, she lived happily ever after.

THE SUN-FISH

THE WITCH IN THE WARDROBE

And so she opened the plank door
Where the dry palm branches had always
Perched, balancing lightly,
Pegged over the architrave;
She swam at once inside a fluent pantry,
A grange of luxury. The silk scarves
Came flying at her face like a car wash,
Then brushed her cheeks and shoulders coolly down—
The fur slid over her skin, oiled and ready,
And a cashmere sleeve whispered, probing her ear,
'We were here all along like an engine idling,
Warm, gentle and alert: what will you do now?'

But when she closed her eyes to feel it closer
Their swatch of sublime purples
Intensely swooping and spinning
Dived past her cooing like pigeons—
Their prickling mauve inside her stretched eyelids—
The bridge was gone and beyond it
She could no longer see
Her body, its flesh without stain, its innocent skin.

A BRIDGE BETWEEN TWO COUNTIES

The long bridge
Stretched between two counties
So they could never agree
How it should be kept

Standing at all
(In the mist in the darkness
Neither bank could be seen
When the three-day rain

The flood waters
Were rising below).
On that day I looked
Where the couple walked

A woman a small child
The child well wrapped
Becoming less visible
As they dodged left

Then right, weaving
Between the barrels and the planks
Placed there to slow the traffic
And something came

A brown human shape
And the woman paused and passed
The child's hand
To a glove and a sleeve

And very slowly
At first they moved away, were gone,
There was the mist,
The woman stood and seemed

To declare something
To the tide rocking below
And for the second time
In all my life I saw

The dry perfect leaf
Of memory stamped in its veins
The promise I heard
Val Kennedy making

At my sister's funeral
In his eightieth year: *She will live*
Forever in my memory. So her words
Floated out on the water consonants

Hardly visible in the mist vowels
Melting and the scatter of foam
Like the pebble damage
On a sheet of strong glass.

I watched the woman,
Memory holding the bridge in its place,
Until the child could reach the far side
And the adjoining county.

ON LACKING THE KILLER INSTINCT

One hare, absorbed, sitting still,
Right in the grassy middle of the track,
I met when I fled up into the hills, that time
My father was dying in a hospital—
I see her suddenly again, borne back
By the morning paper's prize photograph:
Two greyhounds tumbling over, absurdly gross,
While the hare shoots off to the left, her bright eye
Full not only of speed and fear
But surely in the moment a glad power,

Like my father's, running from a lorry-load of soldiers
In nineteen twenty-one, nineteen years old, never
Such gladness, he said, cornering in the narrow road
Between high hedges, in summer dusk.
                                                            The hare
Like him should never have been coursed,
But, clever, she gets off; another day
She'll fool the stupid dogs, double back
On her own scent, downhill, and choose her time
To spring away out of the frame, all while
The pack is labouring up.

The lorry was growling
And he was clever, he saw a house
And risked an open kitchen door. The soldiers
Found six people in a country kitchen, one
Drying his face, dazed-looking, the towel
Half covering his face. The lorry left,
The people let him sleep there, he came out
Into a blissful dawn. Should he have chanced that door?
If the sheltering house had been burned down, what good
Could all his bright running have done
For those that harboured him?
And I should not
Have run away, but I went back to the city
Next morning, washed in brown bog water, and
I thought about the hare, in her hour of ease.

BALLINASCARTHY

Is marach an dream úd Caithness dob' ag Gaeil a bhí an lá.

PÁDRAIG ÓG Ó SCOLAIDHE

There, where the bard Ó Scolaidhe tells the loss
Of the great fight when the Croppies met the Caithness
Legion: the date, 1798, cut in brass,

The man driving the forklift truck said: Keep on
Straight up the road and you'll see the monument
And turn to your right. But when I had gone

Up the long hill to the cross of Kilnagros,
I saw only the spruces that had grown
Darkening green on either side of the stone.

After a mile I turned back and drove west, blinded
By dancing flaws in the light, as I passed
Under the planted trees, like dashed foam

Or the dashes of yellow and white on an old headstone.
Yet in that darkening light I saw the place,
Turned left and followed the falling road

For the graveyard. I searched for my great
Grandfather's name, Charles Cullinane, but I found
Only one Daniel, 1843, one headstone,

And in Kilmalooda I found Timothy's stone
On a headstone in the long grass almost lost,
And Jeremiah's, and I found the name *Bence-Jones,*

1971, cut by Séamus Murphy who made my father's stone
In 1970, in the Botanics, and below that another name
In a different hand, Ken Thompson's, I recognized:

Ken Thompson carves the figure 9
In a different style, as in the stone he made
For my mother and her second husband in their Offaly grave.

I left the Bence-Joneses in the long grass
And drove back to the cross
And downhill again past the secret monument

To the dead of the great battle of Kilnagros
Where the spruces whistle to each other and the carved stone is lost.

THE DOOR

When the door opened the lively conversation
Beyond it paused very briefly and then pushed on;
There were sounds of departure, a railway station,
Everyone talking with such hurried animation
The voices could hardly be told apart until one

Rang in a sudden silence: 'The word *when*, that's where you start'—
Then they all shouted *goodbye*, the trains began to tug and slide;
Joyfully they called while the railways pulled them apart
And the door discreetly closed and turned from a celestial arch
Into merely a door, leaving us cold on the outside.

THE POLIO EPIDEMIC

No hurry at all in house or garden,
The children were kept from the danger—
The parents suddenly had more time
To watch them, to keep them amused,
To see they had plenty to read.
The city lay empty, infected.
There was no more ice-cream.
The baths were closed all summer.

One day my father allowed me beyond the gate
With a message to pass through a slit in a blank wall;
I promised I would just cycle for two hours,
Not stop or talk, and I roamed the long roads
Clear through city and suburbs, past new churches,
Past ridges of houses where strange children
Were kept indoors too, I sliced through miles of air,
Free as a plague angel descending
On places the buses went: Commons Road, Friars' Walk.

A REVELATION, FOR EDDIE LINDEN

Ranged, fanned out—as, in the apocalypse of John,
Those who were not defiled—the victims,
Children, great-aunts, lacemakers and especially
The laborious foreigners, every one
Bearing the emblem of his trade:
How quietly they listen to the lines
Praising their lives, the voice that trembles
Eloquently holding them in place.
The room is upstanding with white pedestals and busts
And a plain, good carpet; there will be coffee soon.
The verses halt and tug. Why do they allow it,
Are they bullied or too modest, can they feel honoured
By the partial mugshot? Here is the coffee,
And probably whiskey in the far parlour
For the famous who stand and stretch.
And I spot you, Eddie,
Stepping back from the spillage,
Imprisoned against glass bookcases
Where the spines in a row slide from *Assyrian* to *Hittite*
(No script more strange, no dragon a more
Outrageous presence than yours) and you draw breath,
Because your retreat is partial, and when you speak
A draught from a city of broken windows
Will come razoring under the door.

ASCRIBED

She sat and wrote as if a voice had spoken, *Write*
For those who never made it to the promised shore
Who waded ahead carrying what they could manage
Above the breast-high flood, the children kicking,
The soft toys saved on their damp shoulders;
How they came to a well-made pillar of stone
Built three centuries back after the Williamite wars
Locked together out of symmetrical stones
Founded on driven piles. And the river spilling
All around it, and the skylarks above a grazing island—

And then the speaking voice was not heard any more, only
The deep gasping of a beast in trouble,
And the voices of the drowned did not reach her at all
But instead it came to her in silence,
An instant: her grandmother remembered in old age
Her long hair down, her wide shoulders bare
Before her basin in the early light
While the cat lapped a basin of fresh milk,
And how as a child she watched without moving.

MICHAEL AND THE ANGEL

Stop, said the angel. *Stop* doing what you were doing and listen.
Yes, you can taste the stew and add the salt
(Have you tried it with a touch of cinnamon?)
But listen to me while you're doing it.
I am not the one who found you
The work in the Telephone Exchange.
That was a different angel.
I am the angel who says *Remember,*
Do you remember, the taste of the wood-sorrel leaves
In the ditches on your way to the school? Go on,
Remember, how you found them
Piercing a lattice of green blades,
And their bitter juice. The grassy roads
That swung in and out of the shade
Passing a well or a graveyard,
The gaps and stiles on the chapel path—
Their windings, their changes of pace
Always escaping the casual watch you kept—
You must go back and look at them again,
And look again the next day, for they change,
There is new growth, or the dew is packed like a blanket.
Later come rose hips and the bloom of sloes,

And you must be there to see them. Your children will find
The sweet drop in the fuchsia flower, swallow it down;
They will run from the summer shower, but your work is to stay,
To hold the pose of the starved pikeman, grasping upright
The borrowed long ladder. After the rain
Dries off your shrinking shirt, the blue flower
Will shine up from the aftergrass where it nestled.
You will have to guess the size of the steam rising,
How it frees itself, sliding up off the field
At the time when the beeches are dropping their mast,
When the sloes are ripe in the hedge, you might still
Find the taste there, among the last of the grain.

SICILY: CERES AND PERSEPHONE

FOR LELAND BARDWELL

The ferry slips like chalk
Leaving its friable mark, like ice gliding
On a marble counter, its shadow melting in the light,
Catania, where the girls in their circle
In the gymnasium held hands,
Embracing, kissing, smiling at me
Like a heavenly ceiling, fading.

What seemed at hand (earth
Blooming with orange-trees and hotels)
When the train rounded the headland was revealed
In shadow, far away
On the other side of the straits.
I can see through a round hole: water
Racing, laughing, and on the dappled ceiling
Shadows in backward flight.

YOU NEVER SAW A BED-END IN A PROTESTANT FENCE

FOR LELAND BARDWELL

There is a film of icy dew over
The spread pastures of Leeson Street.
The dandelions fringing the partitions,
The bunched underwear tossed and dangled
Across nine-bar gates, are flecked
With frost. The Jesuits
Behind walls of transparent mist
Move slowly to their prayers, steaming
And solid, like morning cattle.
Below the street the sleepers are herded
Horizontal in their sofa beds and horseboxes,
The fuzz of ice on their shoulders,
On their tossed hair, not bothering them
At all; the three children going out to school
Whisper and hop between them
In a chink of bus fares.

The area is a breath of cold bright wind
As you climb, holding a child in each hand.
Across the street in 1968
The Garda is still protecting the frozen bus
That carries the strike-breakers to the ice-factory.
The sun lands on him before anything else in the street.
Every inch of his body is tired
As the melting drops on the railings,
On the telephone wires, on the Georgian weeds,
Each one sagging, reflecting the world upside down.

THE FLOOD

I'm out again, straying
Earnest as ever I quested
In search of the neutral ground—
Skirting high fields I look back—
I can still hear the cry.

Did I try this angle before?
The road dips and carries me
Out arched across the Shannon:

Not history, not division,
A pure pouring, out of the north.

The midge's glassed patch, the lark's foothold
Of raised bog, brims, leaks, tilts,
Hithering the trickles merge
In this frosted rush of stasis.

I call on the muscles to shift,
Choose, focus, as if I had found
A crack with a spiral glimpse,
And what lies within. But it comes

Full against me like a motorway—
I can look nowhere else.

Intense, amplified hiss
Of time passing, like nothing . . .
But singular grief:
Repeated, the protest of the mother
By the bed where her daughter lay dead.
The eye can only
Relax, distended:
The heart hammering, the danced tangle
Of light on the sliding depths.

COME BACK

Although there is no paper yet, no ink
There is already the hand
That moves, needing to write
Words never shouted from balconies of rock
Into the concave hills
To one far away, whose hair
On a collarbone resembles
That break in the dunes, that tufted ridge
He must have passed, faring away.

If the railway does not exist yet, there is, even
Now, a nostril to recognize
The smells of fatigue and arrival,
An ear cocked for the slow beginning,
Deliberated, of movement, wheels rolling.

If the telephone has not been invented
By anyone, still the woman in the scratchy shirt,
Strapped to her bed, on a dark evening,
With rain beginning outside, is sending
Impulses that sound and stop and ask

Again and again for help, from the one
Who is far away, slowly
Beginning her day's work,
Or, perhaps, from one already in his grave.

1. *After Drinking the Dragon's Blood*

She is breathless, sheltering
In the shallow architect's
Groove, the last place you'd expect
An echo of faithful speech—
Hearing the voice that taught her
The true note of the wind-harp,
She dashes across, reaches
The wisteria's thick shade
And waits till a sound of hooves
Ambles past the rows of peas
To rendezvous with the badger.

The pigeon as big as a dog
Explains in his shambling grammar:
All this tuning holds back meaning
While setting it free.
                                        Remember,
You were the groom that pushed apart
The weight of two standing horses
Leaning heavy towards each other
In the darkening stable.

2. The Score

Listening to the way that
Everything shakes in his language,
The high wind blown through the tenses,
She feels it keen when the tempi
Settle faster and stricter—
His house is filled up with sound,
A thick rope wound and fastened
Athwart the stairway holds
The walls in place, when the past
Rings in the floorboards. And

Even upstairs the vibration
Penetrates cupboards packed
With volumes of puce-brown paper
Stacked flat; if a triplet picked
On a xylophone enquires,
The knotted silk thread stretching
Snaring the newel-post frays
With the shiver, a verb twists
To a subjunctive, a cat
Rolling over in the sun.

And she ruffles her shoulders:
The cloak she wears, shuddering
Opens out, spreads, a carpet
Made of the loose-woven stalks
Of the Great World-Bindweed,
And every one has a root,
Pierces a trickle, and that
Bleeds downward: hush, the dangling
Strings of glitter hymn the air.

THE SAVAGE

She opens the stopcock and lets it come bubbling up
Filling as far as the reinforced glass floor
And it shines transparent
And is absence that still

Laps with its pulsed currents, the muscles
Like the salmon pushing; as its fizz settles
She gazes in the deep tank, picks out
The shadows meeting, herself; and the long

Quicksilver jaws, and the interlocking lights
Pressing summer and the eye into place,
Remind her of that swatch
She keeps in her pocket (it packs

Every known shade, but when she takes it out
They are all fused into to a glowing white
—So the cloud and the sun fuse, the fish and the waterfall)

—So, was it her arm that sliced
Half a gown away, the silver

Fall, her hand that cut the last line from the letter,
That laid the rooms all open, with their cramped air,
Their claw-footed cooking stoves
And their turned-down beds?

CALENDAR CUSTOM

What is the right name of that small red flower?
It's everywhere, spilling down over the stones
In the sun, every year at just this time.

The colour dims for a minute as the line of dust
Follows the loud white van uphill, and just now
The girls in the bar offer me a glass of water.

What is that soft smell that is everywhere,
The water reeking like tar? and while the cloud
Swells and the rain begins, the man standing

In the yard outside inhales the damp half-hour.
The red is fading again to a pinkish beige;
The plants crouch like cats while it pours down.

The smell is harsher, the light warped panels do
No good, the piecemeal shutters can't keep it out.
Then as his uniform dries to a full blue,

And half of the window brightens, the tall girl throws
The door wide, and the man and the air are allowed
To blunder inside by pillowfulls. She tears

Two pages off the calendar. All colours now
Bright as a mirror drown out the little flowers
Drooping in the soft breeze as their date comes around.

INTERIM REPORT

TO PAUL: NOVEMBER

Dusk and a gate, a leaf
Turning, a dark place:
The cypress-green endpapers
Of a packed book, your filled life.

The ranked evergreens
Frogmarch a slim path;
This enclosure, the blocked tombs,
The crosses, repeat, pinning down

Their instant of focus,
Shuffle the pack, the blades
Of darkness, absence. Peace,
And this is where you were taken.

But you are not yet here,
Still on the move. The orange
Pumpkins you planted are growing in the garden,
The songs you were promised have not all been sung.

UPDATE FOR PAUL CAHILL

Here is the place as you knew it—
The pinned lines of agriculture buckling,
Pressed up against the dark fringe,
The woods, quilting the secret hills.

The one who walks on the high path looks down:

How long will the worker bend
Over the task he knows best,
How long in the ten o'clock heat
Will the one seed twirling on its thread
Disturb the silence?

THE NAVE

Learning at last to see, I must begin drawing;
I cast abroad the line
That noses under stones, presses around an instep,
Threads off into distance and forward again
As it pierces and drags. Like a daft graph it shoots
Up, like a weed falls and rises. I am led, I find it
Looped on every hooked corbel. Drowned in deep shadows
I catch myself in a tangle of rickety laneways,
Part of a procession. The streets
Are full of innocence, a stumbling,
Cobbled bazaar of shining bargain treasures,
Their shimmer resisting the eye.
Remotely the four-four beat of the carnival march
Pulls me aside, adrift on the stepped descent—
A fresh smell from the lemonade stall announces
The square transformed. The trinkets dangle,
Ribbons wrap round and round the coloured poles.
The air darkens, fairylights burst out on wires;
The line calls me upwards, curving banisters,
Their metal studs too nearly worn away,
Come to a point where a little troop,

All brightly masked, waits for more companions
Before the steeper climb.
                                        It is cooler here:
Darkish stone, slate, a marble well, a ramp
With a squashed feather stuck to one side, then old,
Clean tiles. I am drawn, staggering—
It feels like lifting a tall, swaying ship
With wind-filling streamers—
Across the threshold.
                                    And indeed the nave
Hums like a ship, the corded masts and spars
Are tugged by wind, and the uppermost gallery
Swings and revolves. The hanging censer
Vibrates like a spider in his thread. In the rigging clings
A saint whose cure is personal as a song
Performed aloud at a wake by a special call,
Or softly to a patient in her hospital ward.

THE CLOUDS

Octaves higher than the peaks, a skirt of vapour
Hesitates, a press of cloud permits
Globed light escaping, the oriental twirl
I never see without expecting the whinge
Of opening gates. The mountains preen their slopes
For invitations, and a high opinionated
Forehead in profile, as of a woman
With the face of Achilles and the bare
Shoulders of Andromache, gazes—
At which of those barely fashioned heads?

—Searches for one who lives in the moving gondola of light
Spilled on the chosen earth as the ice slides
Off into streams, who lives with people
(For how to do this alone) who are really there,
Having names for hunger and thirst, and like them
(How could it be otherwise) can see across the valley
To where on other cliffs the light
Paints shapes of heads or trees or gables,
So that one hesitates, takes a step back
For a better view, turning, as when the sun struck,
Once, Matthew's counted coins. A new scribal hand

Opening (how else does writing work?) arched ways
To see past the hanging nets, see who is there
In the whirling dance, when you duck and catch:
The moment thinning the curtain,
Real, like the tricks of the light.

THE CURE

They've kept the servant sitting up;
It's late again,
Their fire burning so high they've opened a door,
And from her room

She hears them settling the great questions:
How treat a case
Of green-sickness or, again, one of unrequited love?
The fire burns down,

They close the door. She was writing to her mother,
Resumes: *Don't think*
Of consulting that fraudulent woman. Her sister, who
Died, had the gift.

. . . I understand, it must be hard for her,
So long, no news,
But surely, secretly it comforts her heart
That the child thrives.

The voices boom again, the door is wide,
She hears the bell,
Appears with her candlestick, ready to guide
A guest to bed,

Then back to her letter. *The lady of this house*
Keeps to her room.
The master sighs as he locks the heavy street door.
There is no cure.

THE WATER

Thin as a wash, does it get any deeper
At all, or could we see its depth, since we catch
Only the gleam when the flipped blade
Rewards the light, like a silk flash of hair in the water,

And since our eye muscles are slack as the grasp a bare
Wall has on the sun painting it white?

—Although like the white of dawn hitting a wall this is real
And the floating shards of light are really there—

And O, Hundred-pocketed Time, the big coat lined
With lazy silk pinched close as finger and thumb
Various as oceans, precious-tinted like skies,
What upset you to empty them all at once,
What stretched thread long enough to measure the reach,
A lighthouse searching the dark, scraping the sea with its beam?

WHERE THE PALE FLOWER FLASHES AND DISAPPEARS

Then the waters folded over him
Their long leaves their ripple embrace
Dissolving the lines of his face
The sky crowded on top of him
The trees held the firmament up in its place
Their peacock spread
The last thing meeting his gaze.

The trees began their song the notes
Bound to the spot,
A repetitious air turning again
But strong enough
That the stunned mourners found
They were afoot they had walked outside
In the air although
Just now they felt themselves sinking
Into a grave.

Out of that dark they came and saw the trees
—Branches tense like dancers
Over their glass—they saw the roots,
A piercing grasp
That roved down, under and between the buried stones.

VERTIGO

Shaped like a barrel with asthma, her black skirt
Bunched at her waist, she kneels or squats
At every spot reputed to be holy.
Her two daughters wait and gossip until
She scrambles up and they move a few yards on.

How did such smart women acquire such a mother?
She insists on doing the next bit barefoot. 'Nobody
Does that any more, Mama.' But she's down,
One haunch on a pointed stone, handing the shoes
To the younger one, hauling off the black stockings

Which she adds to the black bag already encumbered
With rosary beads tangled in keys, all the stuff
She's dragged from home. She struggles ahead,
Joining the queue to climb the staggered steps
Along the cliff edge. A puffin lands beside her;

She yelps in surprise. Then she reaches out in her turn
To stroke each of five crosses cut in the slab,
One for the saint, four for his four sisters, named
In the early *Life*. (It was here that he overcame
The crooked landlord and set all the tenants free.)

Then off again. The daughters are resigned
To the last sharp ascent. From below, they keep her
In sight. The mainland spreads in the wide distance;
The clouds are scattering, and above them stands
The stony north face of the abbey, the great door—

But photography barely exists. The lighthouse-men
Have news of the Russian war. The daughters fret,
Watching the bumblebees trample the sea pinks
In the spot where last year a man fell and smashed,
How will they ever get her back down to the boat?

She is terrified of heights. The seagulls' diving call,
The foam at the foot of the cliff, make her feel sick,
But she does look down, and at last sees what is there,
The dimensions, the naming. Yes.
A broad slick widening, an anachronism,

Ambiguous like a leaf floating where never
A leaf has blown, like a word, a calque, swimming
Up into sight through the tides of speech, like a seal
Who plays on the deep ocean: the gate of her days left open,
Her daughters like armed angels guarding each side
Of the path to the edge, where everything pours away.

THE LITANY

As every new day waking finds its pitch
Selecting a fresh angle, so the sun
Hangs down its veils, so the old verbs
Change their invocation and their mood.

Steady through the long gap in the story
A stiff breeze whistles up off the ocean
Choosing a pair of notes, the same key.

A tidal drag sucks back down as deep
As it rode high; the foamy-crested wave
(Astonished at numbers, the white gannets,
In their salt generations) arrives
To listen for that same voice and stays,
Arching smoothly, waiting for the response.

The soaking tears of centuries drill down
Low passages in between the stones,
Keeping to the calendar made out

In columns of names, a single stiff skin
Coiled up and stowed away in the high slit
Above the stone corbel that once had human features.

The wave can pause no longer, called back to Brazil.

IN THE MOUNTAINS

1

You are almost at the end of your journey;
Nobody has asked you for help
Since the child playing by the yellow gable
Who had lost her ball in the gully.
The broad linked chain still weighs down your pocket.

It is early in the mountains,
The mist thronged like blossom,
The grassy road to the harbour
Grey with dew, the branches
Loaded like a bride with embroidery.

2

Do you remember the dark night
When the voice cried from the yard
Asking for water, and you rose from the bed.
You were gone so long, I said to myself at last
As long as I live I will never ask who was there.

But now I want to ask that question.
I see you at the boundary stone and I need
To say the word that will bring her out of the trees:
Notice her: she limps to the field's edge:
A step, a clutch at the baldric, a hand to her hair.

The little stony stream divides forest from field.
She looks away. The wooded scene accentuates
The grace that says *Look—don't look* wavering
Like the spring breeze tossing the leaves, her draperies
Hesitant, her flexed foot on dappled gravel.

THE SUN-FISH

BASKING SHARK, AN LIAMHÁN
GRÉINE, CETORHINUS MAXIMUS

1. *The Watcher*

The salmon-nets flung wide, their drifted floats
Curve, ending below the watcher's downward view
From the high promontory. A fin a fluke
And they are there, the huge sun-fish,
Holding still, stencilled in the shallows.

They doze in their long dawdle foraging at edges
Where warmer streams collide with cold, westward.
Their matched shadows trail them up the sound.
What secretive ocean hid them since last they surfaced
Out of deep *then?* The late bright evening lies
Flat on the sea, they press up against the glassy screed
Or sink to shades in a delicate layer of smoke.

2. *Observations at the Surface*

Tracking tides, traipsing,
Feeding through their fixed yawn,
They have history, patches,
Warm nights with sudden endings.

'The boat was not her measure—
She destroyed the net—
We cut it away and left her
Wounded to death.'

Others were sighted
Passing the Seven Heads
And a year later hundreds
Nose-to-tail off the Lizard.

And again: 'I rounded the corner
In my father's car. They were there,
Exposed, flayed at the quayside,
A bright bloody colour exploding,
Too big for the quay wall,
Too big for the little bay.'

3. Mere Peddling

And again: how fast we forget,
How grimy we see the people: men and women,
The clustered stoves on stony beaches, the various tubs and barrels
Rendering the oil from the liver, sediment
Settling, useful to curriers, ironfounders
And others. The buyers, the carts waiting;
The voice in each one's head that says *Live, live;*
Men able to kill, to impregnate, to hunt
In dangerous boats—'The pale streak over the backbone
Is the place to aim the spear: downward'—
Able to hack cold carcasses and slave
At the hot iron stoves. And when the sun-fish
Had disappeared, to crowd the ships for Ayrshire,
Derby, Cleveland. The women's long cry
The only echo left of all that noise.

4. Their Shadow on the Sea

Krill. Bloom. Copepods. Thermocline.
Elasmobranch. Liamhán Gréine.

In troops of words they form, a gulp dissolves them.
The ocean swathing the globe is a snake mask.

I watch for the outline, widening the maritime stare.
The angles are a scattered puzzle. I will not

Let it take shape yet, trying
To freeze the dappled light and foam.

But they are there already, as the watcher saw them
Once, craning as they nosed in under the cliff,

Suddenly present, a visitation,
Like the faces of my two parents looking at me

From the other side, from the outside
Of the misty screen of winter.

THE COLD

The shrine sunk below the level of the travelled road,
Reached by smooth, icebound stairs and a cramped door,
Holds a single relic in its case of bone.

I have to remember it. Whatever labour, whatever crime
Brought me here, I am warned: I am allowed place and time,
Not a certificate. I stare and commit, but when I try

To draw, the sacristan (and only now I am aware
He is watching) taps on the glass, points to the notice framed
In five strange alphabets. I search for a known phrase:

Only four friendly words open their locks, and those
Are stuck like treasures in the grip of grammar, morose,
Giving nothing away. *Memory,* and then *Alone,*

Memorial, and *Creation.* I am alone here, I can stay
As long as I please in the cold, printing images in my brain,
I can make rhymes and riddles and rehearse them all day,

Around the cracked shapes, the three colours of the stone,
The faces as if through dust returning, the millstone
Hitched in its place, the date according to the old

Calendar, the capitals with sheaves of corn in relief.
The cold invades my hair and fastens around my ears,
And I catch the echoes of all the shifting minds that here

Were braced to carry the same weight. The word that has not been said.
I move out and climb, and the breath of the mountainside
Is a new language, and the stream plunging at my side

In the gully under the bridge has its own word
Which I could almost understand assuming I could hold
Back from inhaling the air of the mountain, and the cold.

IN THE DESERT

Almost day, looking down
From my high tower in the desert:
The sandstorm blows up,
Cuts my tower in half:
A crooked scarf of sand
As high as the window
That looks towards the mountains.
I cover my eyes
With my red scarf that slants
Wrapping my body
And when it is over
I look towards the desert
And I see him again
In the daybreak light
Still walking nearer—
He must be half blinded.

In the desert walking
I see them by the shining,
Reflection of dawn light,
Something bright sewn in the cloth
Worn on the head
Masking the face.
I see them glinting.

He is sand brown,
His clothes brown like sand.
Now he is closer
I see his shadow
As the dawn rises,
A bending shadow
And he nears the well
In the shade of the palm trees.

Coming to the well he lifts
Its wooden covering. Night
And coolness are still down there.
The snakes lie in the well, males
And females coiled together, wet.
Before he lowers his cup to drink
He salutes them saying, happy
Snakes, like the poor people,
Who have only the comfort men
And women find in each other.
Let me fill my cup, let me rest
Here in the shadow.

I hear him praying, I see him drink.
He lies down in the shadow.

THE SCRUBBING MAP

Evening sweeps through the car park, the customers all gone,
When a few old cars arrive with darkness, their tracks
Wide, curving past the daytime grid. They end up
Collected, all facing inward against the far wall.

The drivers get out, stretch, smoke, then sigh and begin
Brushing aside the loose crumple of dirt
Mangled after the day, so as to reveal
A wide piazza with angled flights of steps

Climbing both sides. They brush the treads
Like teeth, clean the risers like a child's ears.
Then moving back across the cleared flagstones,
They change brushes, kneel and begin again—

Prestissimo, as if they were polishing glass,
The stone below discloses all its veins,
The bristleworm's shadow chased into the quarried slab,
All the history of weakness charted, the place

Where the ground gave in or the lettering wore away,
Or the scratched spot where the last one who could read
The frayed relief of graves took a long leave
Of the sunk trace. Now they polish again and gaze

Through a cloudy floor at the place they left behind,
The deep strait that the ferries face at sunset,
And the shadowy patches, where deeper into the night
A few wrecked boats fearfully make their way.

Like rubbed plans their faces look up out of the stone.
Behind their heads are the maps they will make before dawn
Of the way back to their new lodgings,
And where the landlord keeps the spare key, and the butter.

BROTHER FELIX FABRI

The squared interior is tiled
With names, crowded with banners
All bearing devices, twinned
Initials, chequered, quartered.

He feels inside his loose sleeve
For the old bone-handled knife
His grand-aunt kept and used
To pare her afternoon apples;

And trims the square of paper—
He has written all the names
For those at home, forgetting
Nobody who wanted prayers—

He lays it on the tombstone.
He stands upright, harbouring
Such clear thoughts about the roads
He travelled, he might just fall

Asleep. He shivers, picks up
The paper square from under
The crowding feet. And without
Stirring at all from his place

He probes the sleeve again, finds
Flint and steel, and the heads turn
Watching the paper's abrupt
Flame, the names that he carried

By all the harsh paths, returned
Home in a flourish of ash.

THE MARRIED WOMEN

Yes. But you can have no idea
What she was running from,
Feared far more than the convent with its high stairs

It was those women with their bangles
Their stiff new hats at Easter
Their weddings and honeymoons in the Channel Islands.

Their daughters had ponies, the husbands
Had business and whiskey. Their hair
Was crimped in salons, they met each other for coffee

In town after ten Mass. To the child
They seemed made out of timber and steel,
Stiffened by a dose that had penetrated their flesh,

Poisoned and tinged them lightly purple.
She avoided them all her life:
Then on a Monday morning in a pool dressing-room

She saw a woman, that timber face
Her towel as crisp as ever, her jeans
So stiff and brisk on their hook she thought of the new hats.

The woman turned, and under the towel as if
Shrouded by the mantled oxter
Of a heroic bird, was a girl's mother-of-pearl sheen,

A girl's hesitant body, sheltered by the bird's broad wing.

THE LINERS

All the years she worked at sea the liners
Never docked here and, back again on shore,
She watched them anchored at large in the deep water.

She'd sip her bolus of *Stillynight*. The tender swayed,
Bumping the steel mountain. The tall steel door
Was clamped shut and the ship began the turn,

The yellow portholes glowed, the unloaded tender stood away.
The strung lights brightening curved to the prow, the masthead
A star: the waltzing pyramid enclosing all she knew,

Close print of cabins, listed laundry, echoes of command.
It hung like a cloud of midges, like sparks, the bubbles
In her glass. A living face.
                                        The wake spread broad
In the twilight, a smooth wave, a mended scar fading
In a sea of idleness, and the moon skating to her door.

THE SISTER

1

How on earth did she manage
That journey on her own?
When she was a young woman
They had plenty to keep them busy,
They were small, they felt queasy,
They gripped a pillar in the shade
And held on,

And as for leaving home—
Still, the trains have never changed,
They thunder up the valleys,
Built for strapping fellows
Flinging their big bundles
Easily on to high shelves—
Real men.

She turned up at the station,
Small, her clothes, once elegant,
All black. Past the train window
Slid the suburbs, a fast river.

She saw a white-haired man, waist-deep,
Ducking under and rising again—
A cormorant.

2

A lump of a lad handed her bag down to her.
Lopsided she walked as far as the convent door.
They greeted her with a leathery kiss, they told her
Where to find her bed and the hour of dinner.

They knew the silent meal would be no surprise,
No more than the hard bread, tougher at every slice,

Nor the dead silence of night until the first train
Troubled the valley. She would know, lying there,
Others were sitting up, working in pairs,
To finish the stitching, tacking the last of the lace.

But the cold woke her, and a subtle mist, as fine
As gauze, hung on the glass. In the freezing dawn
She dragged a web just as light across her skin,
Veiling herself for good, and she slept on.

CURTAIN

I laid myself down and slept on the map of Europe,
It creaked and pulled all night and when I rose
In a wide hall to the light of a thundery afternoon
The dreams had bent my body and fused my bones
And a note buzzed over and again and tuned for the night.

We advanced to the window: the square frame showed us
Everything, where we had washed up, above rolling domes,
A splash of talk reaching us; behind us we could not hear
How the dark oil-paint slid down the wall
Wiping out the way we had come. The measure changed,

The warped foot staggered, I thought
Of the yelping music, the interval shaken loose,
I will not hear again. The red-haired bard
Rehearsed the bare words that make the verse hang right,
The skewed weights holding in their place like feathers.

THE COPIOUS DARK

She used to love the darkness, how it brought
Closer the presence of flesh, the white arms and breast
Of a stranger in a railway carriage a dim glow—
Or the time when the bus drew up at a woodland corner
And a young black man jumped off, and a shade
Moved among shades to embrace him under the leaves—

Every frame of a lit window, the secrets bared—
Books packed warm on a wall—each blank shining blind,
Each folded hush of shutters without a glimmer,
Even the sucked-sweet tones of neon reflected in rain
In insomniac towns, boulevards where the odd light step
Was a man walking alone: they would all be kept,

Those promises, for people not yet in sight:
Wellsprings she still kept searching for after the night
When every wall turned yellow. Questing she roamed
After the windows she loved, and again they showed
The back rooms of bakeries, the clean engine-rooms and all
The floodlit open yards where a van idled by a wall,

A wall as long as life, as long as work.

The blighted

Shuttered doors in the wall are too many to scan—
As many as the horses in the royal stable, as the lighted
Candles in the grand procession? Who can explain
Why the wasps are asleep in the dark in their numbered holes
And the lights shine all night in the hospital corridors?

ACKNOWLEDGEMENTS

Acknowledgements are due to the editors of the following magazines and periodicals where some of these poems, or versions of them, were published first: *Agenda*, *Aquarius*, *Critical Quarterly*, *Cyphers*, *Dancing with Kitty Stobling*, *Earth Voices Whispering*, *Irish University Review*, *Light Years: a Broadsheet for Pearse Hutchinson*, *The March Hare*, *Nae* (Sardinia), *Poetry Ireland Review*, *Southword*, *Notes From His Contemporaries: A Tribute to Michael Hartnett*, *Something Beginning with P*, *The Stinging Fly*, and *Tsunami* (Trinity College, Dublin).

The author wishes to thank Jim O'Meara, for scientific help with 'The Sun-fish' (which was commissioned by the Calouste Gulbenkian Foundation for an anthology, *Wild Reckoning*, in memory of Rachel Carson); Paddy Bushe, for organizing a weekend on Sceilg Mhichíl out of which came 'Vertigo' and 'The Litany'; Paris O'Donnell, for information about the fifteenth-century pilgrim Felix Fabri. 'In the Desert' copies the snakes in the well from *Arabesques*, a collection of Classical Arabic poetry, translated by Ibrahim Mumayiz (Garant, 2006).